Minding the Gap

All Rights Reserved.

No part of this publication may be reproduced, stored in a retrieval system, or transmitted, in any form or by any means, electronic, mechanical, photocopying, recording, scanning or otherwise, except as described below, without the permission in writing of the Publisher. Copying is not permitted except for personal use, to the extent permitted by national copyright law. Requests for permission for other kinds of copying, such as copying for general distribution, for advertising or promotional purposes, for creating new collective works, or for resale, and other enquiries, should be addressed to the Publisher.

Copyright © Trishka Saffery 2021

ISBN 978-0-9570837-6-9

The right of Trishka Saffery to be identified as the author of this work has been asserted by her in accordance with the Copyright, Designs and Patents Act, 1988.

This book is sold subject to the condition that it shall not, by way of trade or otherwise, be lent, sold, resold, hired out or otherwise circulated without the publisher's prior consent in any form of binding or cover other than that in which it is published and without a similar condition, including this condition, being imposed upon the subsequent publisher.

Published by Jeppestown Press, London.

www.jeppestown.com

Minding the Gap

Trishka Saffery

JEPPESTOWN

Contents

Autumn	5
In the O.K. Bazaars	6
Nonna and Mary	8
Roger	9
Dear Amos	10
Skating with Velkjo	12
Wisteria	13
Cape Town dreaming	14
The Summer I slept with the Communist	15
Lunch on Queen Street	17
Pam 2010	19
Speaking to ants	20
Holding on	21
I should like to be away	22
You held my hand	23
Footsteps in the night	24
Bottle of wine	25
With you tonight	26
On Friday	27
ENDGAME	28
ENDGAME 2	29
Minding the Gap	30
Buddleia	31
Dark horse	32
A cup of tea	34
Kaleidoscope	36
Why	38
Walking with Amos	39
Remembrance Day	40
I thought that I had laid to rest	41
The Collector	42
If I could sing	44

Spanish proverb..45
After the art gallery..46
Reflection...47
Christmas 1986..48
The donkey's story 49
In Maidstone Hospital 51
Mildred and love..52
Mildred speaks from the heart 53
Mildred and God 54
Funeral horses...56
Ghost in Bull Lane 57
Poet at a party...59
Jane..60
Sisters...61
Haiku poem for glass man 62
Murgatroyd Ted...63
Mountain paths 65
Amanda's party 66
Amanda 2012...67
New Noah 68
On hearing bad news 71
Namaan rap 72
Late...74
Carving a song 75
Fear of flying..76
For A.B. 77
Kentwell 78
God in a box 79
God of Huge...80
Salome..81
Sometimes Fear 82
Recipe for a Home-Made Christian woman....................84
Mildred grows older..86
Rock chick..87

Last dance 89
BET YOU WISH YOU WERE ME! 90

Autumn

It was never a part of my plan.
To be fifty-three.
It is a betrayal of the freckled child
Who walked barefoot in the veld
And swore that she would become
Queen of all Africa.
(It was never part of my plan to be fifty-three—
English coldness has eroded and misshapen me)
Five Acre Field lies peeled of hay
Stooks stacked against a Kentish sky;
The cross gleams white on the Pilgrim's Way
And ceaseless, circling seagulls cry.
Sibilant insects stutter and are still;
Long pastures turn to gold upon the hill.
(It was never part of my plan to be fifty-three—
English coldness has eroded and misshapen me).

In Nelspruit now they're waking
To the bird-shout and the shaking
Of great branches and the whirring of wings
And startled whispers of tiny, stirring things.
The sun beats warm on fields of corn,
On vygies, that explode to blood beside the road.
Trees stand half-erased by early morning haze
Where barbet churrs his heart-deep song of praise.
It was never part of my plan to be fifty-three;
English coldness has eroded and misshapen me;
I see the Autumn come, but still my mind
Is stirring with the Spring I've left behind.

In the O.K. Bazaars

On a winter's Saturday
In the O.K. Bazaars,
We watch the lady demonstrator
Attempting to make pancakes,
In an amazing, shining, innovative
Tefal frying pan.
The smell of burnt batter
Is seeping, creeping
Throughout the store;
On a doily are a few oily,
Runny, pitiful pancakes
With lacy black edges.
My grandmother, patience lost,
Has pushed her way forward,
Taking charge; adding flour,
Beating furiously,
Oiling the black-lined pan
With buttered paper,
Talking all the while.
A huge crowd is gathering,
Awestruck, almost fearful,
Shuffling and craning.
A perfect pancake in the air;
It falls back in the pan
Gracefully.
A collective "Aaah" from the crowd.
She hands the shining pan
To the lady demonstrator.
"That," she says, quite kindly,
"is how you do it".

She seems not to see
(As I have done)
The bright, unshed tears
In the woman's eyes.
Later, she recounts the tale,
With self-deprecating humour,
As of a good deed accomplished;
And I, in my child's heart,
Vow that I will never
Become my grandmother.

Nonna and Mary

Nonna and Mary after lunch in the mealie-scented hut
Heads bent over the creamy palm; tiny coloured beads
Licked up by the darting needle, weaving messages of love
And loneliness and pain; each colour an ancient code.
(No-one warned Nonna not to love her;
Nonna dreamed Mary was her mother)
The old black crone with pendulous breasts brings mussels
That gleam wetly in the basket on her head. They race
To meet her. *uMama* they call across the dunes; "our mother".
Later, she tells again the story of the ancient shipwreck.
(Her own father had seen all the sailors drowned;
Many Spanish bodies, Spanish jewels were found.)
Mary and Nonna are afraid of snakes—
And of the old white witch
Who keeps her glass eye in a bowl on the dusty windowsill.
But, sometimes, in gingham dress and bonnet, Nonna goes
With Auntie to tea in that paraffin-evil old house.
(Nonna reassures Mary that witches can't
Poison small girls at tea with their aunt.)
And once a green mamba slides by Nonna's small bare feet
And the tall black body holds her strong and still
Until it passes. And Mary holds the night at bay
Rocking her and crooning softly *Thula, thula baba.*
(No-one warned me I ought not to love her;
Nonna dreamed Mary was her mother.)

Roger

Roger was brown, burnished and bright,
He laughed and lived with all his might;
He was our hero, our little Adam
The human link between Sophie and Madam.
Sophie would iron and scrub and sweep
While Madam would chase and tickle and tease
Until, at last he'd fall asleep,
Sprawled in my pregnant lap, at ease.
My son was born; Roger turned two;
We did what the law required us to do—
He was sent to the Homelands, somewhere or other
To be cared for by an old aunt of his mother.
Each month, from her wages, money was sent;
Reports filtered back it was not being spent
On Roger; protests, letters and then the train
Journey; Sophie, disquieted, back again.
We have word that Roger is starving, ill
And the white doctor insisting the bill
Be paid in advance; I send a letter—
I'll meet all costs; just get him better.
But ignorance, greed, White laws have won;
"Oh, Madam", she whispers, "We've lost our son."
So we wept together, so sad and wild;
And where her poor, dark head was pressed,
Sweet milk for my own well-nourished child
Ran like blood across my chest.

Dear Amos

Dear Amos, I am writing this letter
Because the shrink here says it's better
Out than in.
He says that by confronting the past
I may be freed of it at last;
So I'll begin:
I was confused about my skin
From a very early age;
It had a distinct lack
Of black
And I would fly into a rage
At suggestions that it might
Be better to be white.
I remember when my nurse came on the bus
With me, she would take without fuss
The back Black seat reserved for her kind,
But, Amos, I was the one who would mind
And shout aloud that it wasn't fair—
And all the white faces would turn and stare;
For I carried this guilt they did not share.
Even at six, I did not feel right;
I'd done nothing to earn being white.
And, at boarding school, I would far rather
Die than shout out "Muntu" or "Boy"
To a waiter older than my father;
(Insults were used with spiteful joy
By spoilt young girls to serving blacks
Not born the white side of the tracks!)

And later, Amos, people I knew
(I was at University with Hugh,
Slept with Marius, friends with Rose)
Were arrested, tortured; do you suppose
I've spent my life making reparation
For the sins of an entire white nation?
And, if I have, were you a part
Of the payment plan; this giving my heart
To men who could only give back sorrow?
I'll bring it up in the Group tomorrow.

Skating with Velkjo

It was early evening in the winter half-term
I had gone with my stepfather to the Olympia
In Johannesburg. Old, cold, draughty, the ice rink
Was damp carpeting, warm feet, hot popcorn, loud voices.
My head down, I circled the shining ice, placing my feet
With care. And, crossing my feet to turn, I stumbled
Now and then, not yet at ease with this new skill,
My heart thumping with excited concentration.
Then, just as I heard the song, he came across
The gleaming ice, waltzing, twirling effortlessly;
Ah, mein lieb Elisabet thundered the heavy waltz
And my stepfather, with such grace, such smiling
Courtesy, stopped before me, holding out his hand.
With his other hand across my back, he guided me,
Expertly, into my first real waltz, gliding, turning.
And suddenly my feet knew what they should do
And I was smiling, smiling, smiling;
Understanding at last
How it feels to be a daughter.

Wisteria

Wisteria;
All the length of the pergola,
Hanging grape-like
From broad blackened beams,
Spilling down the walls;
Great lilac and white bunches
Above our heads
And below the dormitory window.
Wisteria,
Sweet in Johannesburg sunshine.
And the quick, light footsteps
(Not allowed to run)
On the flagstones
And the warm burr
Of the lawnmowers
On the grassy terraces
Between the loquat trees.
The heat,
The smell of wet leaves,
And grass; the dripping wisteria,
In sudden summer rain.
And the voices
Of the young girls;
Their laughter
Still sounds in my ear,
In my heart,
On a summer's day
In Kent.

Cape Town dreaming

The old woman's head is full of dreams tonight;
Beaches, rocks, the small, shared flat
Where the spring tide, at its height,
Would sometimes wash against the door.
And the small black dog called Nothing
Barking at the waves.
The Atlantic coldness of the pool between the rocks,
Just about wide and deep enough to slide into
On a baking Sunday afternoon,
Having eaten, daringly alone, Sunday lunch
At the tea room on the main road.
And somewhere there was a young man;
Sad; badly stuck together, but her friend.
She remembers that they made a pact,
When he left to travel to California;
If neither one should meanwhile marry,
In ten years, they would come back
To that beach—and meet again...
And they would marry one another.
And, by then, they would not care that lust
Was the no part of the glue that held them;
Friendship would carry them through...
But she never did go back.
And now, she cannot remember his name.
But the dry warmth of that day,
The light,
The bright sand, his strong hand
These
She remembers.

The Summer I slept with the Communist

That Johannesburg summer of 1963
Was the summer I slept with the Communist.
In the half dark, candle-lit coffee bar;
Somewhere in a side street of Hillbrow,
The flare of that untamed copper hair,
The wide swift movements of his hands.
His laughter; the turn of those thin wrists
Pulled me across the room
To stand quietly in front of him.
I cannot think now what I said,
But he left the comrades at the table
And we walked quietly, pressed close together,
Through the darkened streets
That led to my small flat.
That summer now seems to me to have had
Endless mornings of sunshine;
Flowerpots blazing with orange nasturtiums
On the narrow balcony;
And evenings of passionate political talk,
When I would listen, question; nowhere close
To real understanding.
And sometimes I lay beside him in the night;
With his thin ribs beneath my hand
And I would ache to understand the heart
Of this gentle, driven man.
There were always leaflets, poorly hidden
Around his small room,
Frightening tales of close encounters
With the Special Branch,
And anxious visits to his comrades,

Driving along small, unmetalled roads.
I remember playing with the children
(It seems there were always young children)
I would draw with them; tell stories,
To distract them
From the urgent, often angry voices
In another room; always speaking,
It seemed, of retribution,
Bridges, bombs, plans, schemes.
Revolution.
(And myself, nowhere near to understanding.)
In the end, I moved
A thousand miles away; then six thousand.
And the whispers came down the years;
Pretoria Prison. Two wives lost.
And his child.
Then cancer, and his death.
And my heart squeezes,
Remembering his beautiful smile, that hair;
And still I am nowhere near
To understanding…

Lunch on Queen Street

We had lunch on the verandah
Of the Portuguese coffee shop,
Dipping the fat, oily chips
In periperi sauce.
Thick smells of Jo'burg; dust and diesel
And sweet warm bread.
Flies, everywhere; circling, intrusive,
Disregarding the absent-minded
Flicking of wrists and fingers.
My mother feeling hot; blinking
Her half blind eyes
Against the sunlight
That glinted
On metal and glass
From taxis and passing cars.

Strange that I cannot now remember
Whether my mother
Wanted hot milk or cold
With her coffee. I remember only
My graceless, teeth-grinding irritation,
As I changed the order and waited
For the fresh jug to arrive.
And a thousand unnamed hurts
Battled suddenly at my throat;
And I could hardly speak
To her.

Down the steps and to the left; the less

Hazardous route back
To her small bungalow.
She clutched my arm tightly.
I warned of obstacles, holes
In the crumbling pavement,
That she could not see.

And sprawled by the door of the barber shop,
The drunken, friendly Zulu
Called out greetings to us;
Honouring us as mothers.

Pam 2010

It seems that my mother
Has come
To the end of herself.
The child has gone
Who peeped and smiled,
With the still beautiful
Blue eyes,
That now can see
Only edges, partial faces;
Slices of light.

She feeds the forbidden cat
Dried cat food,
And sneaked morsels of meat
From her lunch time plate,
Rattling onto an old saucer
In her silent room.
She lies on her bed,
Stroking the compliant cat;
She sees, often, she tells me,
Her long dead mother
And her sister. Who talk to her.

One elegant, languorous hand
Unceasingly strokes the stubby fur
Of the kitchen cat;
And I stand wordless
At the edge of this chasm
Of unfathomable loss
That lies between us.

Speaking to ants

My mother spoke to ants;
Small, black kitchen ants
And larger, wine-coloured battalions
As they boldly marched across
The wooden kitchen table,
In search of breadcrumbs, sugar,
Sometimes, home-made jam.
Like a kindly enemy General
She would explain to them
That this was all
That they could have;
In the morning, they must be gone.
Her voice would be soft, but clear;
Determined.
By morning, they would be gone.

But she never addressed the termites.
Yellow, orange, they spread like pus
Across the floorboards.
Poison or boiling water
Would despatch them.
And, in those moments, to me,
A child, she seemed
Strangely ruthless and angry;
Frighteningly unlike her kindly self.

In later years, she spoke to cats,
But they remained somehow aloof,
Regarding her as a Mad Old Woman
Who spoke to ants.

Holding on

All my life I have held on
Too tight;
And then, at the very moment
I should have held on,
I have opened my hands
And the world has slipped
From my fingers.
All my pain I have held
Too close
And then, at the very moment
I should have held my tongue,
I have opened my mouth;
And the agony has slipped
From my lips.
All my loves I have held
Too tight;
Then some perversion of despair
Makes me hurl them in the air—
And they take flight.

I should like to be away

I should like to be away
From this cold country,
Moving into winter,
And go where the rich smells
Of cut grass and sprinkled suburbia,
Buzzing softly in the sunshine,
Can catch at my throat.
I should like to be away
Where the rough fingertip veld
Spreads thickly as sardine paste
On. the gentle gracing hills;
I should like to be away
Among the rich brown smells
Of soft mid-afternoon rain
Dropping on the jacarandas...
But, instead, I shall hide myself
In the safe, familiar bosom
Of your distaste. And dream
Of better days.

You held my hand

You held my hand
And something passed
Between us, palm to palm;
You held it tight
As if you never would let go
Something passed between us
Palm to palm, tonight.
You held my hand
As if it were yours to own
And later when I was alone,
I could not understand
The way I found
Myself still bound
As if you held my hand.

Footsteps in the night

Footsteps in the night,
To me, were no problem.
Woven into the warm tapestry
Of childhood bedtimes,
With murmured voices, dishes, coughs,
Soft laughter and a smell of cigarettes,
Were footsteps in the long passageway,
The kitchen and the bedrooms.
Aunt, brother, grandparents, dog
Make distinctive counterpoint
To my own soft breathing
As I lie in my mother's huge bed,
Stroking the satin covers,
Counting, tiredly, the plaster grapes
Upon the patterned ceiling.
And, sometime in my sleep,
My silken, perfumed mother
Rolls tiredly into bed,
Late home from her work on the radio;
She murmurs and is asleep
Breathing through her mouth
Soft puffs of Kolynos.
Lord, help me find a way in this darkness,
Where my experience cannot lead me;
Show me how to reach the children
Who hear, in terror, footsteps in the night,
Coming up the long stairway;
And the furtive, whispered affirmations
That they are Daddy's
Special little girl....

Bottle of wine

Listen, God, here I am at forty eight
And it seems like my kids can't wait
To leave home and move in
With friends, or live in sin
With most peculiar young men—
And I want to know, Lord, when
The last of them have left the nest,
What am I meant to with the rest
Of my life?
I was a good wife
To Ron—and you know he was a sod,
What with the fear and the pain, God,
Towards the end.
So I've lost my best friend,
God, and now the kids are going too—
And what am I supposed to do?
Listen, Lord, I've got a sort of prayer
Or perhaps it's a dream, where,
In time for Christmas, You send me
This feller; he's fiftyish and six foot three,
A widower, handsome and romantic
And of course, Lord, he is frantic-
Ally in love with me and brings
Gifts of chocolates and other things;
A rose; a poem; a bottle of wine…

No, I can't cope with all that crap.
Listen, Lord, how about if we scrap
The feller? Just the bottle of wine
Would be fine.

With you tonight

With you tonight,
I found myself
Suddenly, childishly,
Wanting to touch, to stroke,
To capture the texture of you—
To feel your face beneath my palms
And breathe your warmth.
Your amused eyes
And the half-smile
About your mouth
Told me that you knew this:
So I wonder if you laugh at me
For knowing all that I know
And yet behaving like a fool;
Or, wryly, at yourself,
For knowing all that you know
And never behaving like a fool.

On Friday

On Friday when, at last,
You're gone away
I shall feel no more sadness
Than I feel today;
There will be no compounding
Of this inward pain—
The silken threads between us
Will feel no added strain:
How shall mere miles unman me
When you are able
To set continents between us
Across a wooden table?

ENDGAME

I came across this headline:
COMPUTER CRACKING CHESS—
BY STARTING FROM THE ENDGAME
And, for a blinding moment
I saw how I might crack Life
By starting from the Endgame;
But seconds later
I malfunctioned
And found that I had lost
The entire programme.

ENDGAME 2

I have been pushing this thought
Around my mind;
That if there appear
Too many answers
To just one question
Is just one answer correct—
Or are we asking the wrong question?
I think I have come back
To the point
Of trying to crack life
By starting at the Endgame.

Minding the Gap

Forever minding the Gap.
Always, it seems, leaping
From one life, (no time to waste)
Into another.
Always minding the Gap,
But sometimes the Gap cries out,
Demanding attention;
More strident somehow than even
The imploring call from
The latest destination.
Mind the Gap
Mind the Gap.
I think I may have devolved
Into being that Gap
That you are better to mind.

Buddleia

Buddleia has declared herself National Flower.
She proclaims ascendancy from the railway
Tracks and the urine-foul redbrick backs
Of disused shops in the old towns. Her hour
Has come in the neglected suburban garden beds
Where she grows huge on graceless legs
To pull into the scented centre of her power
The sycophantic butterflies:
I say her manifesto is all lies.
(Vigorous, vulgar, immediate, debased;
Wasteland, buddleia-strewn, still is waste.)
My soul clings to something half-remembered, fine;
Forget-me-not, primrose, violet, columbine,
Lady's slipper, cowslip, clover, broom—
(Protea, cosmos, aloe; and, ah, the koraalboom).

Dark horse

God always had top billing – the Superstar,
But, granted that they were both crowd-pleasers,
The one that really pulled them in at Christmas
And at Easter too, was Jesus.
So there was the Father, Christ with his Word
And then the Holy Ghost; a rather poor third.
Somehow, He lacked stature—a shame
That He didn't even have a proper name
Like Jehovah, God, Creator, or Father,
In fact the whole thing was rather
Badly done, from a PR point of view.
Take Jesus now; at least you knew
(Even if it sounded like a fable)
That He was the one born in a stable
And that He had quite a way with water,
Both for walking on and making wine;
That He drove the Devil from the Grecian daughter
And was indisputably Divine.
And there was the matter of the fishes and loaves;
And cripples taking up their beds in droves...
What I'm saying is at least you knew
Who this Jesus was, who had died for you.
And God, though perhaps a little remoter,
Was still the choice of your average voter;
Creation, Commandments, Noah's Flood,
Adam and Eve, sacrifice, blood;
He was the one with the Power and the Glory—
But the holy Ghost was a different story.
He seemed, somehow, a nonentity;
The one Jesus said 'Will come after me',

And we seemed to have no clear directive
About Him, but, to be quite subjective,
I had Him figured as really kindly, and yet
If I'm really honest, a tiny bit wet.
Then, praying, once, in a moment of calm,
I truly felt His presence, knew His balm—
So now (though I've not much to lose, of course)
I am placing most of my faith on the dark horse.

A cup of tea

The sleepy cat stretches, sun-soaked
On the draining board.
Speculative, spiteful.
She dumps the cat upon the polished floor
And wipes away the film
Of fur and yellow sand
And mites;
Speculative, spiteful.
"I wish that you would keep that cat"
She calls, in her light, white voice
"Out of the kitchen,
When I'm not here".
The man slumps bleeding in his chair
Before the television,
Where her shining voice has cut him
Like diamonds.
He is watching some Ethiopians
While they die
For John Craven's Newsround.
She moves decisively about
Her mint green kitchen,
Deft as a blind man, in this space
She inhabits and does not see.
Now the kettle makes a whining
Counterpoint
Against the turning and the churning
Of her mind
And the clicking of the high red heels
Upon the gleaming floor.
Presently, smiling her ancient hatred

Through pearly, even teeth
She lays before him
A perfect cup of tea.

Kaleidoscope

It seems there has been
Some manner of
Implosion.
This Word
Has inwardly
Fragmented me
And I must
Reassemble
All my parts
Into a new whole.
I am become
A kaleidoscope
To the world.
Twist me
Shake me
My pieces lie
Illumined
With new beauty
Thus
Or thus;
But lacking
Perfection.
Yet sometimes
The pattern
Will lie clear
And true
For a long
Moment;
Then the world
Picks me up—

And
Shakes
Me.

Why

Why should it make you upset
That once I had a lover
Whose name I now forget;
Why is that a threat?
My dear, I remember the name
Of his sorrow;
I remember his sadness and shame.
Tomorrow and tomorrow
I shall carry his poor sadness;
He will remember that I was kind.
So, if names are now forgotten,
Why should we mind?

Walking with Amos

Your face adorned with moonlight,
We walked in silence on the shining
Pebbles, amongst the stretching shadows.
Sometimes we heard the shuffle of sheep,
Or geriatric panting of hungry hedgehogs
Behind the silver-berried bushes;
Sometimes the only sound
Was our footfall on the pebbles
Walking, not quite in step, together.
We turned back, before we reached
The end of the road:
I think we will always, my dear,
Turn back.

Remembrance Day

Eager boys in baggy camouflage
And stout brown boots invade
The shopping precinct.
They synchronise large watches
On bony, adolescent wrists;
Cheerful, self-important.
Ebulliently, they thrust the brimming
Boxes of bright paper poppies
At old women in checked coats
And cheerfully rattle tins
At pink-cheeked teenage girls,
With long blonde hair
And brightly patterned leggings.
Giggling, repartee and the clunk,
Clunk, clunk of coins;
Blood red poppies bloom on chests
Of the band fit for heroes.
A boy with an unfinished face
And the broad, expectant grin
Of all of those
Formally-photographed generations
Of doomed youth,
Stands before me with a flower.
I press some silver in the slot
And hurry away, my head averted;
Breathless with despair.

I thought that I had laid to rest

I thought that I had laid to rest
All the worst (and all the best)
Of what I'd felt for you, my dear;
Then tonight, with no warning, I swear,
The heart burst upon me like a shout
And all that I could think about
Was my need to touch your face again;
And all my peace has turned to pain.

The Collector

I am the Collector
The catcher and snatcher
Of incidents and incongruities,
Scenes,
Odours,
Faces,
Places,
Dreams,
Fragments,
Trifles,
Bright moments of time,
Emotions,
Laughter,
Cataclysm;
I catch them all
And push them into the holes
Inside my mind
And into the dark hollow
Beneath my ribs
Where I store these things.
When all my space is filled
To bursting,
I assemble my collection
From the available pieces,
Selecting,
Arranging,
Polishing;
Seeking perfection, precision,
To hand you, with infinite love,
My life upon a page;

Again.
Then, for a while,
I can use the raw places in my mind
To think,
And I am freed to love;
But I am the Collector...

If I could sing

If I could sing,
Might it have been different;
Might my pain, in clear, pure notes
Have poured from my lips
To form miraged cathedrals
Upon the air
Above my emptied self?

But poetry's elastic, draws out pain
That, viciously, shoots back again.

Spanish proverb

Take what you want, say the Spanish;
And pay for it.

Ask what you want, says my God—
And pray for it.

But I never ran this by you, Lord,
Nor stopped to ask your will.
I reached out for that glittering prize;
Prepared to pay the bill.
But the prize was never truly mine
And the cost was time-delayed:
So I have loved whom I would love—
And paid.
And paid.
And paid...

After the art gallery

There, in the train,
Somewhere between the art gallery
And Liverpool Street,
Came the beginning of understanding.
Pressed by the five-o'-clock crowds,
(They tired, unsmiling,
Arms upraised, clutching straps
In mute, commuter surrender)
We stood together, unspeaking.
Your retreat was a palpable thing;
The closing of eyes,
A small drawing in of elbows,
Slight down-tilting of your head;
Some inner turning out of lights
In all the great, bright rooms
Of your mind.
My eyes touched your face;
Appraised some fine thinning
Of the skin, some pallor,
A few lines—
And the smallest droop
At eyes' edge and mouth;
So little outward change
In my friend
For this passage of forty years.
But, perceived my heart,
This man
Has lost
All his bluebell woods.

Reflection

She looked into her mirror tonight
And found that, in the course
Of driving to the timbered shop
And in the course of smiling,
Smiling. smiling while the women
Parade like young princesses
In the white and cream bridal gowns,
Scarred with sequin and pearl
And stiff with luxury;
And in the course
Of driving herself home;
And in the course
Of selecting a pre-cooked dinner
And toilet paper
At the supermarket;
She had transmogrified.
In the mirror, she saw
Only a black outline of herself,
Like some woman
In a children's colouring book;
Or a caricature.
And she pressed her cheek
Against the cold glass
And wept again
For the one who was not there
To colour her in.

Christmas 1986

Tonight I will make a poem;
Pink satin words of love,
Curled and teased and pulled
Into a bow; a sweet confection
To the eye and ear.
The gift itself is somewhat
Unpromising,
Being the sweepings
Of forty-five years
Of compromise
And doubt;
And now this latest cataclysm.
But I will most sweetly
Parcel up for you
These sweepings of my life;
Trying to disregard my fear
That when the dust has settled
The floor may not be there.

The donkey's story

Being, myself, a mother,
I made some sense
Of the soft murmurings
And the sudden, sharp
Intakes of breath
From the young woman
And the curling and uncurling
Of her fingers at my neck;
I blew softly on her face
To comfort her.

I, too, needed comfort,
After the long, cold journey
That had ended
In this unfamiliar place.
There was food. And water.
But much of the manger ledge
Was taken up with sleeping places
For my master and the mother.
And, now, for this birthing.

How tenderly she wrapped Him
In soft cloths to keep Him warm;
How sweetly put Him to her breast.
(I could see this clearly,
For a strange, sudden light,
From the hills beyond Bethlehem,
Turned the night sky—
And this lower room—
As bright as daylight.)

And I could hear—
(But not as I hear shouts or curses)
—I could hear
Such sounds of worship
Borne on the cold wind
As I had never heard
In Nazareth.

And later, there came shepherds;
Sweating, muttering, excited;
No, something beyond excitement,
As they gazed
On the swaddled infant
And fell, at length, silent,
To their knees.

And I hold that moment,
Now, in my heart.
For this was when I knew
That I was born
Not merely to serve my master,
With the carrying of wood
And the tools of his trade.
I was given life
That the Saviour of mankind
Might have safe passage
Upon my back.

In Maidstone Hospital

Once I was numbered,
Dear friend, upon your hand;
Counted.
Counted upon.
It seemed I was as vital
As any other digit
Of that powerful hand—
And my own hands flew apart,
Without question,
To give you my soul.
This morning I woke
In pain, dreadfully afraid,
In this darkened ward;
Totally helpless beneath
The great tide of fear
That battered me.
Later, I became aware
That the terrible emptiness,
The dismemberment,
Were not, in fact,
Surgically caused.

Mildred and love

Mildred just spent the last year giving
Her middle-aged love to a slightly odd
And altogether unattainable younger man
And all she will say is "Thank God,
I hurt—therefore I'm living!"
Once, she told me, he'd held her hand
But, as far as I can understand,
He looked on her as an older sister;
She wanted him unable to resist her.
Oh well, that I suppose is la vie!
But, darling I wish that you could see
The tea towel he brought her back from Cairo.
(She'd rather hoped for a naughty Biro,
Where something rude emerges from the sand
When you upend it in your hand;
Or perfume, or a desert rose)—
What sort of man, do you suppose
(I mean, knowing Mildred)—what sort of bloke
Gives her a TEA TOWEL—except as a joke?
They used, she told me with some defiance,
To canvas together, for the Alliance
And go to barn dances, run jumble sales;
Go out to dinner; but Mildred fails
To mention if they ever went to bed:
In the end—you know me—I just up and said
Whatever happened, Mildred—was he gay?
She just smiled and said, "No, not every day."

Mildred speaks from the heart

I am failing, I am folding
My taut springs have come unfurled.
I am become some ever-shrinking
Little friend of all the world.
I am reaching out to stroke you
With an ever-weakening arm
And every blow that falls upon you
Strikes me; I take the harm.
I am bending with your burdens
I am bruised with so much care;
I am become the unseen victim
Of your pallid love-affair.
Please listen, will you hear me—
My whispered desperate call;
I am folding, I am failing:
Hold me close against your body—
Or I fall.

Mildred and God

Mildred has spent many years
Trying to get hold of God,
But He's bloody elusive.
She's been to the most exclusive
Cathedrals, where you might expect
One of His calibre to hang out;
But He's never been about;
And to small down-market chapels
In the East End, just in case
He has been slumming—
But He's never shown His face.
(Although, once, the scent of His aftercare
Was still hanging upon the air)

Mildred has this theory about God—
That He's an early riser;
(She insists that the imprint of His hand
Often lies upon the wakening land)
She also swears He has a sense of humour,
That He plays celestial peek-a-boo;
That, just when you think you've seen Him—
Look again—what you saw was you.

Mildred's left dozens of messages
On His twenty-four-hour Answerphone
Asking Him to get in touch
But of course she's never really known
If, when she seems to get a reply,
It's coincidence, or answer as such.
Then, suddenly, last week, He called.

After all these years, she was bewildered;
There was this sort of voice in her head;
"Hello. God here. Yes, Mildred?"
And, almost choking with happiness, she said,
"Thanks, God, for calling. It's daft, I know,
But I've needed to hear You say 'Hello'."

Funeral horses

I saw four funeral horses
Black and glossy as dowager's velvet,
Braided, bridled and plumed,
Neat-stepping in the busy road
That goes through
The council estate.
They pulled behind them
A dusty farm cart.
Three country travellers sat aloft,
Dressed, not for a funeral,
But soberly, for outdoor work.
And they passed close by me.
I drove home, heavy-hearted;
Believing I had witnessed
A prophecy.

Ghost in Bull Lane

Tonight, when the chill came down
With the day's end
And I felt the cold crunch of leaves
Beneath my homeward feet,
I remembered Bull Lane.
My children not yet teenagers,
Excited to be out in the darkness,
We had said our back-door goodnights
Through puffs of misted breath
And followed down the long path
The meandering beam of our small torch.
So, we turned into Bull Lane.
It started, I recall, with the smell
Of cigarettes, sharp upon the air
All about us.
And then the sound, close by,
Yet falling on some inward ear,
Of whistling;
The tune was *Lili Marlene*.
A whispered question to my children.
Yes, they could hear whistling,
But did not know the tune.
We saw no-one, yet we knew,
All three together,
When he had gone past.
Now, on a night such as this,
My thoughts go to that young soldier.
Will he still be swinging down Bull Lane
From the war-time army camp,
Cigarette in hand,

Whistling the same bars of *Lili Marlene*,
I wonder, when I, too,
Am long dead?
And will he give a friendly wave
As he passes
The three of us?

Poet at a party

How do you talk to a Christian poet
Particularly one so uncompromising?
(Does he not know that compromise is oil
To the workings of women's lives?)
I suspect that he has put in his order with God;
A Christian woman, Lord, well-educated,
Non-smoking, who does not eat
The corpses of animals.
(And, Lord, of a height and weight
To look good beside Your Poet...)

How do you talk to a Christian poet
Who has so tamed and trimmed language
That the dark forests of his heart
Are become merest topiary?

How do you explain to a Christian poet
(Particularly one so uncompromising)
That, whilst you may have some attributes
Upon the list he lodged, this is clearly
Not a match made in Heaven;

(Your own well-presented request to God
Never having included
A poet.)

Jane

Certainly, there had been evolving
Some rumbling certainty of change;
Something developing, expanding.
Perhaps there would be complete
Transmogrification?
A disguise? A costume change?
Or simulated flying, involving
Harness, pulleys, cable, counterweight?
Pointy toes on a stage-lit swing?
But I was totally unprepared
For sudden and total disappearance,
Without, at least, a thunderclap,
Or billowing stage smoke.
I did not expect this utter silence;
Not a trace of echo.
I did not reckon
On just one Act
And no curtain call.
That was not the script, Jane.
Not at all.

18.01.2019

Sisters

(For Virginia, Denise, Wendy, Jill, Ronnie, Janey, Carlynne and Jacobeth;
and for Daphne, Iris, Dora, Maureen and Mrs C)

Sisters, now I've lost a few,
I know they're not, like shining dew,
There every morning. Ah, no.
You hold your sisters—and let go;
Sometimes too fast—or painfully slow.
Sometimes your sisters move away
And you are left to watch and pray;
And sometimes sisters softly fade,
Dissolving from sunshine into shade,
Quietly, sweetly, unafraid...
So, sister, if my touch seems light
Upon your soul, please understand;
I am afraid to hold you tight—
And have God open up my hand...

Haiku poem for glass man

Glass man. Shattered
By the too high note; bleeding
From shards of his own mind.

Murgatroyd Ted

While rummaging at a sale last year,
I heard a faint whisper, tinged with fear
From a tiny, straw-stuffed Teddy Bear
With a hole in his cheek and a ragged ear,
"I'm Murgatroyd" and he shed one tear;
Please won't you get me OUT OF HERE"...
So a hero changed hands for five new pence;
His size is small, but his heart immense.
Brought up in Mayfair (well known at the Ritz)
He led six dolls to safety during the Blitz,
Through a gap in a central heating vent
(And this is how his ear was rent)_
Hospitalised for the rest of the War
In a Children's Ward—where the things he saw
Led him to form a minstrel act
With a one-eyed dolly—and it's a fact
That they toured the wards, night after night,
Bringing the patients joy and delight.
Then a changer in his fortunes came about;
After the War, came the sorting-out.
He was bundled up with the hospital toys
To be sold at a fund-raising fete for 'Our Boys'.
Bought by young Master James for a copper
(A well brought-up boy and discerning shopper)
A sunny nursery with his own little chair;
And, in the night, a warm pillow to share.
But years went by; Little James was Jim
And preferring others in bed to him.
Then packed in a box, put under the stairs;
Dust-choked dreams for years and years.

Then tossed on a table in a Village Hall
Amongst broken soldiers, defenceless and small—
But full of pluck, with an air of mystery
That proclaimed "I'm a Bear with a History".
Now he rules from a cushion on my bed;
Even the CAT respects Murgatroyd Ted!

Mountain paths

There are paths that flank the lower slopes;
These grow ever rougher, steeper, ever colder,
Lifting slowly, towards a misted mountain top.
Circling the great unfriendly mountain,
There are paths.

There are journeys shared, taking no account
Of the final destination; walking so close
That the place ahead, where steps must sharply
Diverge, stays hidden from our minds.
There are two paths.

They are not so far apart. Sometimes we wave,
Or bravely shout. But grassy slopes give way
To unfriendly woodland. And the voice
We think we hear may be no more than
The creaking of old branches.

And suddenly, a patch of wintry sunshine
Lights the mountainside. Now, it seems,
Treading separate paths, we have come far
Along our journeys, almost within sight,
Nearing that unknown mountain top.

Now, there is some sunshine dancing, a little
Forlornly, on the sharp pebbles ahead.
And, although the paths will not join again
Before the end, the soft wind carries our voices;
And that is sweet.

Amanda's party

Tonight there is a party
For Amanda.
We have made sixteen giant pom-poms
Of lime-green and fuchsia;
Each requiring eight sheets of tissue,
Cut separated and teased
Into shape with patient hands.
Cocktails, non-alcoholic , and in shades
Of lime-green and fuchsia,
And decorated with paper umbrellas,
 Will be handed to arriving guests.
There will be a buffet,
All home-made by our best cooks;
Canapes, little squishy things; pastry
Wrapped round small pink prawns,
Asparagus, mushrooms;
Creamy dips with delicate crackers;
Small cakes with brightly coloured icing,
Candles, streamers and music.
Thirty teenage friends
And members of her family
Will talk and eat and laugh and dance,
Served by smiling women
Moving quietly between them,
Passing, fetching, clearing.
Amanda is sixteen;
But this is not a Birthday Party.
It is our way of thanking God
That she has finally had the all-clear
From Cancer.

Amanda 2012

We have lost
Amanda.
Full of courage
Full of promise.
She has quietly
Slipped past us
And is running now,
Joyfully,
Without fear
Or uncertainty,
In green, green places
With fuchsia-coloured sunsets.

New Noah

Somewhere in rural Yorkshire
A farmer named Thrupp
Is building an ark.
(In the hospital of a nearby town,
He was christened Jonah at his birth,
Being a sickly infant
And thought unlikely to survive;
But in recent years he has changed
His name by deed-poll
To Noah.)

Noah, as befits a hill-farmer,
Is a strong and practical man;
The ark is almost halfway to completion.
He has been following an ancient design
Found through an archaeological Internet site.
Noah is acting on clear instruction,
He says, from God.
He began building the ark twelve years ago
Following the first great storm
In Britain. He has been advised by God
Of worse storms still to come.
God has warned him that, in the final great storm
Of November 2024,
The seas and the rivers will flow
Together and the whole of this land
Will be covered by the waters.
Noah and his two sturdy sons
Have been collecting pairs of animals.
He has made further use of the Internet

To compile an illustrated list of British species
That must be represented
On the ark.
He was astonished to see how often
'Extinct' appeared on the lists,
Whilst being slightly relieved
That it made his job easier.
(There is a rumour that the Council
Is considering prosecution, on the grounds
That he is keeping a zoo
Without permission. Or licence.)

Noah is a good man.
He takes in good spirit the market-day
Laughter and the jibes of his fellow-farmers,
Most of whom are childhood friends;
He reminds them that only last week
There were 52 flood warnings in England.
In the midst of all his certainty,
Noah is faced with one dilemma
He has two Friesian cows, Rosie and Daisy
And a fine Friesian bull, Gestapo
(So named for his vicious unpleasantness)
Daisy, unusually in a farm animal,
Has become a household pet.
No longer fecund, she lives out her days
In the fields and barn,
Calling at the back gate to moo softly
For attention; for the stroking
Of her soft nose and ears.
Noah would like to take his Daisy
And Rosie on the Ark
And leave behind Gestapo;
But he knows this is not God's will:

And that Daisy will be forfeit.
Scratching her gently between the ears
He explains in a soft and tender voice
(At odds with his great farmer's body)
Why he will have to betray her.
What he cannot foresee is that,
Two days later, he will suffer a stroke,
While heaving timber onto the ark;
And die instantly.
He cannot foresee that the farm,
Nearing bankruptcy from neglect,
Will have to be sold at auction.
He cannot foresee that the menagerie,
Amidst great press speculation
Will become the property of the RSPCA
And the WWF.

He cannot foresee that Daisy and Rosie will go
To the slaughterhouse;
Only Gestapo will survive, sold on:
And only God knows
What will happen
In November 2024.

On hearing bad news

Absurd to say, but I always knew.
Now, I wish that I could dance with you
Gently, on some deserted pier,
At Bridlington, or somewhere near.
Just shuffling in the semi-dark,
My hand held close beside your heart.
And sometimes we might quietly sway
With the weight of all we cannot say.
And my adulterous soul, still weeping
With all the secrets it's been keeping
Would touch your face, wish you farewell;
And climb back in its cracking shell.
And you will move on—and I will stay;
Sad echo of one, long-past day..
(Ah, double pain and double cost
To lose again the one I lost.)

Namaan rap

I am the Commander, the topmost brass—
Salute me, soldier, you're saluting CLASS
I command all the armies of Ben-Hadad
And Benjamin is my Grandad.
But there's just one thing that frightens me;
And the name of that thing is LEPROSY!

(I'm a simple girl and an Israelite,
Captured by Syrian soldiers one night.
Now I am maid to Namaan's wife
And the old guy's leprosy troubles my life....
What we're talking here, friend, ain't Urticaria—
This guy needs healing by the prophet from Samaria!)

Now I heard what this little maid had suggested
And it seemed like time the truth was tested:
With a letter from my king, new threads, some gold'
I set off to find the cure she'd foretold.
Seems there's some hassle between the two kings
But I don't bother my head with all those things—
And with horses and chariots off I race
Till I stand, at last, by Elisha's place.
So I am waiting for the guy to come out to me,
Pray and lay on hands, miraculously
So my flesh will be cleansed of the leprosy;
But I tell you that AIN'T the reality!
He just sends this little servant out to me
Who repeats the Prophet's recipe:
"Seven plunges in the Jordan is what you require
And your flesh will be back as you desire".
I almost can't hack it, but I've nothing to lose,

So, with a few choice phrases, I take off my shoes
And start splashing round like a right banana—
And suddenly the guys are all shouting "Hosanna"
And my skin's turned as soft as a baby bird's wing
And I am shouting out "Hosanna" to the King...
I am the Commander, the topmost brass
Salute me, soldiers, you're saluting CLASS
I command all the armies of Ben Hadad
And Benjamin was my Grandad.
One thing will never again trouble me;
Praise God, I've been healed of leprosy!

Late

My brother is late.
No, not dawdling
Nor wandering
Amongst his family trees;
Big, African LATE.
And by his death
So much becomes,
Quite simply,
Too late.

Carving a song

I want, Lord, to carve you a song
From a wood sixty eight years long
And wide as cold Atlantic sea;
Polished, restored by an alchemy
That passes understanding.
I need help, Lord, to smooth the grain,
Restore colour, remove the stain;
I need bits of tar from passing ships,
Old rot and mildew, gouges, chips,
Removed, by the Carpenter's sanding.
I want to carve you a song, Lord,
Refined by a craftsman's knife;
I want you to hear with a smile, Lord,
This song that is my life...

Fear of flying

Last night, I dreamed that I could fly:
Not hurtling, like Superman, through the sky
But lifted in the air by the strong steady beat
Of huge. church-art, feathered wings, neat
Between my shoulder blades, but spanning
Twenty feet outspread. Riding the air, fanning
Small clouds from my path, I soon grew brave;
I executed a somersault, a triple-axle and save
For losing a few small feathers here and there,
I cleaved with triumph through the air.
I began to pass people I thought I knew
Or slightly remembered, who sighed as they flew
By and were lost in the soft shining fluff.
Then, just as I felt that I'd had enough,
Who should fly by but Judas, quite old,
Smiling strangely, his teeth capped in gold
And I passed a fiddler who I think was Nero
And that Waco leader, like some super-hero
Competing with Hitler to attract a small crowd;
But most who flew by were just weeping aloud.
Later, awake, I came to understand:
Hell is flying free—with nowhere to land.

For A.B.

Dear friend, from out upon the street
I hear the drummer's first, soft beat
And then the fiddler makes a sweet
Clear opening trill.
I close my eyes, but still
I cannot bear, dear friend, to hear
The answer from your tapping feet
I cannot look, nor catch your eye,
Or trust myself to say. goodbye;
For women know these ancient tunes
That stir men in their mothers' wombs;
To such a tune, man leaves his wife,
Dancing, prancing from her life;
And young men dance off to a war
And never dance back any more;
To such a tune the young and brave
Dance upon their fathers' grave;
To such a tune, heard in the night,
You dance from all that's true and right.
Outside there is a strange parade
Of children, whirling to the tune
But, though they dance, they seem afraid;
Each holds aloft a black balloon;
An old man plays a silver flute
A frightened baby starts to wail—
And, underneath his pristine suit,
The fiddler flicks his pointed tail.
You clap and grin, arch and spin;
A girl runs down; she's joining in:
Friend, if I leave, I am not bored—
But God forbid I should applaud.

Kentwell

This morning will not be diminished
Because I am here alone:
With a lover's eye, I have seen
Swallows skirling from the moat wall
And watched the widening circles
Where the carp rise;
I have traced the track of a lone coot.
Since the first light I have been here;
My heart's hand has stroked the great oak
And caressed the mossy bricks;
I have watched the thinning of the mist
Upon the water
And the laying down of soft shadows
On the grass.
I have looked gently on ancient roses
And hanging hedges
And stood silent where the new calf
Lies curved against her mother's flank.
I have heard from the first note
The sweet swell of bird song
And felt some measure of its beauty
And its pain:
This morning will not be diminished
Because I, alone, have seen it—
And for all that you have given
To those I love, to me;
I give it thee.

God in a box

My friend has sometimes felt
That God is in a box,
But I have no such delusion.
I know him in sunlight, fields rocks,
In the cherry tree's profusion
Of heavy snow-flake bloom;
Not in churches, although, years ago,
On a Xhosa mission station
He was in a tiny whitewashed room.
And once I had an acute sensation
That he looked at me, so,
From a face I passed in the street.
(But I was carrying my sense of defeat
And missed the moment
To take up my life and follow Him)

God of Huge

I rejoice in the God of Huge.
The Creator of Worlds
The Maker of Galaxies,
Suns, planets and stars
Beyond numbering.
I rejoice in the God of Huge.
Architect of untamed mountains,
Plains, deserts, oceans,
Canyons, caves
And impenetrable forest.
I praise from my soul
The God who breathes life
Over elephants, eagles;
And scuttling scorpions.
The Artist who paints the zebra,
And the humming-bird;
Makes velvet the deer antlers.
I praise from my soul the Engineer
Who created me.
Who gave the lion
A voice to shake the jungle
And the sweetest song of praise
To the blackbird at my door.
Oh, God of Huge,
For the blackbird alone
I would love you.

Salome

Was Salome perhaps misunderstood
For doing what she thought she should?
Where was she coming from? In the palace,
Was she feared and hated for her malice—
Or was Salome merely thought
A rather spiteful, silly sort
Of teenage girl, pretty but dumb
And firmly under Herodias' thumb?
Was she really cruel and mad;
Or simply showing off to Dad?
Did pubescent hormones seal the fate
Of the sainted head upon the plate?
Perhaps her instructions were misconstrued—
Or her fragile mind had come unglued?
Did anyone give her a proper chance
To say she did not care to dance...?

Sometimes Fear

Sometimes Fear,
Soft-footed as a panther,
Will slide into my early-morning kitchen,
Wanting to be fed titbits
Of left-over failure.
Or, stretched across the doorway,
He watches my every move,
As I drink the first coffee,
And softly kneads the silver carpet
With his ivory claws;
So that I am unable to pass.

Sometimes Fear
Like a familiar lover
Whispers into the endless grey of night
But such a telling litany of loss,
That I, too, become completely lost,
Stumbling towards my God
In the painful iron clogs
Of Hope Deferred.
"Abandon Hope", smirks Fear
Flexing his ivory claws:
So that I am unable to pass.

Sometimes Fear
Like a crooked showman
Will hold a distorting mirror to my life,
Mocking friendship, history, family,
Until truth becomes unrecognisable
And everywhere I look for God

I see only my Munch-like screaming face
Reflected back to me.
And Fear will roll upon his back
Extending his ivory claws
So that I am unable to pass.

Sometimes Fear
Can be outwitted; outperformed,
Made to step aside at last
Until, hungry and disconsolate,
He will slink shamefaced past God,
And lope towards his former jungle home
And I will shout at his retreating back;
He promised that He would always be with me;
He is still with me.
I will not be afraid.
So I am able, at last, to pass...

Recipe for a Home-Made Christian woman

Here's how you bake a Christian woman
Starting out from scratch:
(If the first one is successful,
You could always try a batch).
They are really very wholesome,
Though they haven't got much taste,
But kids and animals like them
So nothing goes to waste.

Take one slightly shapeless body
And wrap in medium white skin
(Or you could use beige or brown
If it's important that they sing...)
Add a tablespoon of middle-class—
Blue-collar just won't suffice—
And several pounds of sugar
(So they are really, really NICE)
We normally add two broad feet,
For the wearing of Jesus sandals
And a pair of strong, child-bearing hips
(Embellished with love-handles)
The hands are MOST important—
Use the kind for multi-tasking—
So they can Hoover, bake and baby-sit
Without your even asking...
Add a splash of Jesus-babble
A pinch of martyr-at-the-stake;
Remove stray bits of humour;
And bake, bake and bake...

Apparently, now my local church
Has this Ready-to-Serve variety;
A lot tougher than your Home-Made...
And short on Proper Piety;
All claiming to be Daughters of the King!
(A very poor substitute for the REAL thing!)

Mildred grows older

Mildred (and this is what I'm told)
Has some problems with growing old.
Mildred (The Tough) Mildred (The Bold)
Does not fear Death—she hates getting old.

Mildred's cornered the market in Being Wise,
Telling it like it is, eschewing lies;
So to her this has come as a ghastly surprise;
Not the outward change—but the inner demise.

Her heart isn't broken; it's not turned to stone.
(Often it rings like an unanswered phone)
But she wishes she might somehow have known
That her heart could mature to this no-go zone.

She wants to tell God that it's not from choice;
She certainly loves him, but to clap and rejoice
Is an effort of will, always tinged with remorse,
(For her God deserves so much better, of course).

Lord, you know Mildred; she is everywhere,
Trying to do right, doing more than her share,
Her sense of duty endorsing each choice;
God, help the Mildreds to hear your voice.

God, help the Mildreds who have stood aside,
Help all the Mildreds whose hopes have died.
Lord, bring them close beside Your throne—
Show them this truth; they are Your own.

Rock chick

I see her walking,
Where the stream emerges
From beneath the dirty bus station
And flows slowly past
The faded Deco grandeur
Of the old car showroom,
To drop down noisily
Sliding into the mother river.

All afternoon the soft snow
Has been painting white
The old, tiled roofs;
Frosting the parked cars
And small town gardens
Beneath the grey, grey clouds.

(Woollen hat, bright with colour,
is pulled below her ears.)
The blonde hair escapes
And blows against her face.

This is a true blizzard.
Snow, in soft flakes
And small, icy droplets,
Swirls and gathers,
Sways the guitar case, clutched
In her bright gloved hand.

I see her walking.
The neat, booted feet,

The blue, checked coat
And the guitar,
In the cold, cold wind;
The swooping of the snow;
And I long to paint
Rock Chick in a Blizzard.

Last dance

Will you dance with me?
Some early evening by the sea's edge,
Shall we chase that last, long
Sunlight on a lonely beach?
Where the smooth-baked sand
Cracks beneath our softly sliding feet,
Shall we silently dance together,
Without music—and with no words
To fly into the salt air
And fall to shards between us?
And shall you hold my hand,
Palm to dry palm as we move
To the whispered rhythm
Of the distant waves.
When you dance with me
My hand is light upon
Your shoulder; yours, dear friend,
So gentle at my back.

Before our hearts or lives divide
Before that final outward tide
Would you not take another chance
And join me in a long, last dance?

BET YOU WISH YOU WERE ME!

I bet you wish you were ME!
Standing here without a care...
With her badly dyed hair
And, frankly fat...
But, apart from that,
I bet you wish you were me
I bet you wish you were me
With great holes in her
memory...
But I'll tell you what
I'm quite sure I was HOT
About 1953
I bet you wish you were me!
I bet you wish you were me
As I carelessly laugh
At all the hard graft
With husbands and lovers;
I'VE a world full of BROTHERS;
I BET you wish you were me...
I bet you wish you were me
A poet and actor;
(Though the flatulence factor
Does not enhance
My attempts at dance...)
I bet that you wish you were me...
I bet you wish you were me
Unlikely daughter of a King
But here's the thing;
With the love of Jesus and time
You could be standing where I am.

I bet you wish you were me
I bet you wish you were me
Standing here in my wide-fit shoes;
If you're ten or sixteen or twenty-two
I get to see Jesus
WAY before you...
I bet you wish you were me!